I0374781

Original title:
Threads in the Wind

Author: Mariana Leclair
ISBN HARDBACK: 978-1-80586-128-7
ISBN PAPERBACK: 978-1-80586-600-8

Weaving Light in the Air

A butterfly flits by with flair,
Tangled in bright, wobbly hair.
"What's this?" it giggles with glee,
A ribbon lost, just like me!

Kites spiral up high, strings all a-twist,
Dancing to tunes that no one can list.
A squirrel interrupts with a silly grin,
"Count your yarn balls or you'll never win!"

Sunbeams weave jokes in the breeze,
While bread crumbs float like tiny unease.
Chasing them down, a cat takes a leap,
Only to land in a pile of sheep!

So here in the chaos, we all take a chance,
Laughing and spinning in wild little dance.
Join the parade of the quirky and bright,
Weaving our laughter in pure, silly flight!

Tangles of Memory and Space

In a closet of thoughts, things get tangled,
Old socks and lost keys, all quite mangled.
A hat that once winked on a sunny day,
Now an awkward reminder of 'what went away.'

Balloons with a wink, they drift up too high,
Chasing after dreams as they float in the sky.
A mix-up of moments, all caught in a bind,
Laughter echoes softly, old tales intertwined.

Ethereal Weavings of Emotion

In a loom of delight, I stitch up a grin,
Wooly thoughts leap, like little kids in.
Each thread has a giggle, each knot a small jest,
As my heart purls joy, never needing a rest.

Laughter like confetti, it flies through the air,
Snagging on memories, some light, some rare.
With a flick of the wrist, I unravel my fears,
And weave them in patterns that dance through the years.

Stitches of Light and Shadow

A needle of sunshine darts in and out,
While shadows do prance and twist all about.
Each stitch a bright chuckle, a playful slight,
In this fabric of life, I find pure delight.

Ducking and dodging, a thread does a twirl,
As I trip over shadows, oh, what a whirl!
With laughter like sparkles, the scene brightens bold,
In the garments of mischief, my stories unfold.

Spirits Among the Fibers

Ghosts of my past hang out in the seams,
Whispering tales, twisting my dreams.
A sock that seems haunted, with a laugh and a jive,
Dances in corners, oh how it's alive!

Knots of confusion play tricks on my head,
Each smile a fiber, where mischief is spread.
With playful apparitions, I thread and I sew,
In the fabric of folly, my heart's all aglow.

Unraveled Stories

A sock flew by, on a quest for fame,
It tangled with a shirt, declared its name.
“Let’s spin a tale of missing pairs,”
As pants took flight, beyond all cares.

The hat chased after a gleeful shoe,
Together they danced, like a merry crew.
With each gust of laughter, they soared and twirled,
In a whirlwind of silliness, joy unfurled.

The Metaphor of Woven Winds

A scarf once lost, now found with flair,
Tickled the breeze with its silky hair.
"Let's take a spin," it giggled aloud,
While a mop looked on, feeling quite proud.

A feather so bold joined the frolicsome dance,
Swirling around like it stood a chance.
With each gust of giggles, they danced on air,
In their own little world, a most quirky affair.

A Symphony of Untangled Lives

A trio of bows began to conspire,
Whipping through breezes like strings of a choir.
"Together we'll sing in the bright sunshine,"
As they juggled their notes, oh how they'd shine!

A noodle forgot it was destined to dine,
Twisted through trees making friends so divine.
The lettuce looked shocked, the tomatoes they laughed,
In this dinner turned circus, joy's never daft.

Lyrical Twists Above

An umbrella flitted with whimsical cheer,
Chasing a dandelion, fluttering near.
“Come dance with me, let’s spin through the blue,”
As the clouds giggled softly, their laughter grew.

A paper airplane soared, full of high dreams,
Misfired its launch, served up silly schemes.
With each twist and tumble, the giggles did roll,
In a sky full of jest, they conquered the whole.

Whispers of Silken Ties

A spider spun a tale so grand,
It caught a fly, then waved its hand.
The fly wore shades, began to sway,
"Not another web! Let's dance today!"

A breeze blew past, with quips so sly,
They twirled and twirled, oh me, oh my!
The air was filled with laughter's call,
As bugs and threads enjoyed the fall.

Dance of Frayed Edges

A cloth with corners torn and worn,
Decided it would not feel forlorn.
It gathered scraps, a crazy crew,
Shimmied and jived in the morning dew.

A button popped, it laughed aloud,
"We'll form a club, let's draw a crowd!"
With patches bright and colors bold,
They wiggled like they were pure gold.

Breeze of Forgotten Connections

Old socks met gloves, a pair quite odd,
They chuckled softly in the thick fog.
"Remember me?" the left one said,
"I lost my mate and felt half-dead!"

They reminisced of days gone wild,
When feet and hands danced like a child.
The wind picked up, with a giggle so fine,
They twirled together, feeling divine.

Weaving Dreams Amongst the Leaves

A leaf fell down with a twisty spin,
Wishing to dance, let the fun begin.
It called to acorns, each snug and round,
"Let's form a band, where joy is found!"

They rustled together, in breezy delight,
Crafting a song that soared to great height.
Their laughter echoed through trees so green,
As they spun around, a whimsical scene.

The Essence of Channeling Airborne Echoes

Balloons in a frenzy, oh what a sight,
They wander and giggle, giving all a fright.
Chasing a wind that tickles their seams,
Floating like laughter, dancing in dreams.

A kite with a mission, it flies like a fool,
Trying to impress, oh what a tool!
Its string sings a tune, a whimsical beat,
As it dip-dances low, with not a care to greet.

Woven Serenades of the Myriad

Socks on the line, they flail and they wave,
In a daring display, no normal life they crave.
Caught in a tussle, old topsy-turvy,
They shout for the breeze, 'Come twirl us, we're nervy!'

A napkin takes flight like a bird on a spree,
Whirling and twirling, oh can’t you see?
With crumbs in tow, it flirts and it flaps,
Bringing the chaos of lunchtime mishaps.

The Dance of Celestial Ribbons

Streamers adorned with bright little dots,
Bouncing and swaying, oh what funny thoughts!
In a swirl of colors, they plot and they plan,
To tickle the clouds like a mischievous fan.

A paper airplane, with ego so bold,
Thinks it's a jet with a story untold.
It crashes and giggles, a tale of its own,
In a world of laughs, it's never alone.

Lacing Moments with Solitude

A lone feather flutters, with secrets to share,
Seeking adventures, it floats through the air.
It lands by a puddle with glee and a splash,
And giggles at ducks who quack and they dash.

In an empty park, a leaf blows a kiss,
To the breeze and the trees, in a moment of bliss.
It waltzes along with a whimsical grace,
Making nature chuckle, in this funny place.

Echoes of Woven Ghosts

In a town where fabric sways,
Old garments dance in playful ways.
A sock escapes with a cheeky leap,
While shirts perform their brand-new sweep.

Cloaks whisper tales of yarn and thread,
Spinning stories of the half-dead.
A button rolls while cracking jokes,
As hats debate which one provokes.

Scarves twirl as if they're alive,
Arguing over who can dive.
Stitch markers giggle in their game,
Each one trying to earn their fame.

Frayed hems complain of their life woes,
While zippers compete, each one shows.
Laces tangle in a lively chat,
Good luck finding the lost combat!

Secrets Carried by Gales

A breeze with secrets starts to play,
Whispering yarns in a breezy way.
A caper tosses hats with glee,
As wigs take flight like kites at sea.

A gust of laughter twirls in spins,
Weaving mischief beneath our skins.
A pom-pom rolls off in sheer delight,
While wafting giggles dance in flight.

Scarves get tangled, having fun,
As jokes take off, they're never done.
Puffs of wind trade silly lies,
As socks form pairs that aren't so wise.

Layers flounce with a dash of sass,
While spools of thread plot, none will pass.
In this wind of whimsy, we abound,
With secrets carried, all around!

Fragments of Forgotten Stitches

A needle's lost in a world of woe,
Where patches tell tales of fun long ago.
Mismatched buttons form a cheerful crew,
With stories of laughter stitched through and through.

Forgotten fabric recalls the dance,
Of sleepy socks in a sleepy trance.
A stitch unravels with a sudden snort,
Creating chaos, a comical sport.

Patches giggle, they're all a mess,
Competing for title of the best dressed.
With seams that sigh and hems that tease,
They weave their dreams carried by the breeze.

In a quilt of giggles, they find their home,
Where loose ends twirl and threads will roam.
Each fragment sings of days gone by,
In a patchwork world, they laugh and cry.

The Fabric of Uncertainty

In a tapestry of silly doubt,
Lies a secret we can't live without.
Threads argue over who is best,
While garments jest about their quest.

Cloths slip and slide, making a fuss,
As they drape around and start to cuss.
A strange mix of patterns leads the way,
Where plaid meets polka-dot in disarray.

Baffles of fabric slip and slide,
Finding humor where stress would hide.
An apron grins at the wildest stain,
While shorts debate if it's all in vain.

In rows of colors, chaos thrives,
With patterns clashing, life survives.
This fabric of oddities makes us grin,
As we embrace the madness held within!

The Journey of Unseen Pathways

With wobbling steps, we stroll along,
Avoiding potholes and righting wrongs.
Our shoes are squeaky, our plans are grand,
But off we go, as fate has planned.

A squirrel darts by with a nutty grin,
While we chase laughter on a whim.
A compass spins, we make a turn,
In this bizarre world, there’s much to learn.

Steered by Ghostly Tides

A boat that sways with whimsy's breath,
Prodding the past, defying death.
The captain's a cat with a crooked smile,
He steers us forth in ghostly style.

With each wave's chuckle, we dance anew,
A puddle of laughter, these waters pursue.
Chasing shadows, making a mess,
Oh, what a joy, this jolly distress!

The Intertwined Paths of Chance

Two forks collide, a pickle's twirl,
One leads to laughter, the other to swirl.
They blink at me like cheeky sprites,
As I wander in whimsical delights.

A parade of ducks in top hats march,
While an impromptu dance brings joy to arch.
Life’s silly game of hopscotch glee,
Leads to the places we didn’t foresee.

Glimpses of Silk in Twilight

As daylight wanes, the colors blend,
A tapestry of mischief has no end.
Silk echoes shimmer with laughter's bite,
We chase the moon in the fading light.

Beneath the stars, giggles abound,
Funny echoes of joy resound.
With every twirl, the world feels right,
In this playful dance of the twilight night.

Awakening the Silent Clouds

In the morning's gleeful light,
Clouds burst into silly flight.
They dance and wiggle, twist and shout,
Making rainbows all about.

The ground squirrels giggle in surprise,
As fluffy forms drift through the skies.
A pancake cloud made a funny face,
While sunbeams join the merry chase.

When wind whispers with a cheeky breeze,
It pulls the clouds with utmost ease.
They tumble, roll, and bump in flight,
Like playful puppies in delight.

So let's applaud this airy show,
Where laughter swirls and breezes blow.
With every puff and playful sigh,
The sky's a clown without a tie.

Crafting Whispers in Motion

At the stroke of noon, skies giggle,
The sun's bright rays give clouds a wiggle.
Like cotton candy spun so fast,
Each puffy shape is at a blast.

They've dressed in hues of pink and blue,
Looking like marshmallows fresh and new.
A breeze tickles, they start to dance,
Frolicking as if in a trance.

One cloud chases another so sly,
As if the moon blinked, 'Oh, my!'
Each twist and turn is full of cheer,
As if they waved to those down here.

And when the sky fills with delight,
It's really just a frolic fight.
So gaze above with joy and glee,
For clouds are funny, can't you see?

The Flight of Elusive Fibers

In the realm where the breezes tease,
Fibers frolic with the playful freeze.
They swirl and twirl, go wild and free,
Like a circus caught in jubilee.

Each strand has quirks, a comical sight,
Drifting far into the vivid light.
They squabble over who can glide,
And tumble down like they’ve all just cried.

Oh, one claims it’s the master of flair,
While others argue, twisting in air.
They tickle leaves, bounce off the ground,
With giggles swirling all around.

So watch them float and surely grin,
These playful fibers with mischief thin.
For in their dance, joy takes a stand,
As laughter circles, hand in hand.

Softly Singing the Sky's Threads

The sky hums a silly tune,
As clouds parade in afternoon.
They swish and sway with a happy cheer,
Like marching bands we all hold dear.

One cloud suggests a game of peek,
While another plays the hiding freak.
They puff and puff, then burst in bursts,
In jolly antics where laughter thirsts.

A breeze joins in, a sly old joker,
Stirring up mischief as a coaxer.
“Let’s race to the horizon's end!”
And soon they spin like playful friends.

So lift your gaze and start to laugh,
At nature’s own light-hearted staff.
For in this playful, silly show,
The sky and clouds share joy and glow.

Tethered to the Air

A sock took flight, oh what a sight,
Dancing with glee in morning light.
It twirled past the cat with a playful meow,
While birds in the sky raised a curious brow.

The breezy whim made a kite feel shy,
As it tangled up high in a butterfly's tie.
With laughter erupting, the neighbors all stared,
At the flying laundry that nobody prepared.

Mistrals of the Past

Once a hat flew, right off a man's head,
Chased by a dog, who found it quite red.
They raced down the street, like a whimsical race,
While onlookers chuckled at the silly chase.

A shirt from the line took off like a jet,
Zooming through gardens where flowers could pet.
It whispered of secrets, old laundry remarks,
And wished for a home among the park sparks.

Flights of Woven Dreams

A scarf with ambition soared high in the zone,
Tangled in branches, it moaned a soft groan.
It wished to be free, not caught by a tree,
While the squirrels just stared, as if they could see.

A napkin has lofty goals to achieve,
To dance with the clouds, if only believe.
It flutters so freely, a whimsical snack,
In dreams of a picnic, no crumbs to unpack.

Knotted Tales in the Breeze

Old shoelaces reminisced with a sigh,
Of races they ran, oh how they could fly!
But now they just dangle, all knotted and frayed,
Laughing at memories that won't ever fade.

A belt from the closet felt bold on that day,
And leapt from the drawer in a jazzy display.
Twisted and twirled, round the lamp it spun,
While the purse just giggled, ‘This isn't much fun!’

A Cascade of Ephemeral Linkages

In a world of tangled yarn,
A cat thinks it's a charm.
Chasing colors with delight,
Slippers flying in mid-flight.

The grandma knits with speed,
Knots erupting like a seed.
Her dog is stuck in a ball,
Rolling round, he can't stand tall.

Laughter echoes through the room,
As Grandma's yarns begin to bloom.
A scarf for someone? Quite a race!
But it’s a hat – that’s no disgrace!

The dinner waits, but who will serve?
A sweater now, with so much nerve.
In chaos, they find their fun,
A dance of fibers, life undone.

Threads of Destiny in the Breeze.

A kite escapes with no remorse,
Tangled high in its own course.
Kids below laugh at the sight,
As it dances in pure delight.

A ribbon caught in a squirrel's plan,
Twisting here, then off it ran.
Nature giggles at this game,
While the trees stand tall, no shame.

The wind declares, 'Come one, come all!'
Twirling scarves around the ball.
It’s a party of bits and bits,
With laughter and a few funny fits.

By sunset, the colors fade,
Yet in memory, the fun is made.
Tomorrow brings more chance to play,
In a whirlwind dance, come what may.

Whispers of the Unraveled

A tangled mess upon the floor,
The cat has claimed it – just one more!
As yarn escapes her playful claws,
She pounces, creating quite the cause.

Unraveling thoughts catch the breeze,
A sock on the line, if you please.
It flails like it's got a mind,
A dance of fabric, whims unwind.

The neighbor shouts, 'Will it ever stop?'
As I hang on to my crochet prop.
My stitches flying with the bees,
They're crafting jokes between the trees.

As darkness falls, the laughter fades,
But memories of frayed parades.
In mornings, I'll start anew,
With a wink to the chaos, that's my view.

Dancing with Frayed Edges

A scarf too long for its own good,
Waves hello to the neighborhood.
While half the town shakes their heads,
It tickles toes and makes new beds.

Grandma's pants, oh what a sight,
With patches sewn in sheer delight.
A fashion statement? Who can tell?
Who would guess they fit so well?

The squirrels debate, in hasty twirls,
How to snag some shiny pearls.
As buttons pop and threads go wild,
The forest laughs, each creature smiled.

But in the end, it's just a cloth,
That weaves together giggles, froth.
Embracing every little flaw,
Life threads softly, and we draw.

Time’s Winding Yarn

Life’s a spool around we twine,
Lost my grip, oh how divine!
Hiccups, giggles, stitches fall,
Mismatched socks, we wear them all.

In the drawer, chaos reigns,
A knitted cat in tangled chains.
Purls of laughter, knits of fun,
Who knew yarn could weigh a ton?

Unraveled dreams and playful snags,
Chasing laughter, dodging rags.
In this fabric, joy ablaze,
Life's a sunny knitting craze!

So if you feel a little slack,
Remember, love’s the real hijack.
As we knit through every day,
Dance with yarn - it's time to play!

A Celestial Crochet

Stars are beads on sky’s vast net,
I’ll crochet a sun, you bet!
Moonlit threads of silver shine,
Comet tails in playful line.

A cosmic hook in my hand,
Whispers of space, oh so grand.
Aliens laugh at my design,
“Daisy chains? Yours or mine?”

In galaxies of tangled lace,
I stitch a love, a warm embrace.
Knots of fate, they twist and weave,
Even aliens can't believe!

So let’s crochet amidst the stars,
Forget the doubts, forget the scars.
With every loop, let spirits soar,
In this universe, there's always more!

Fading Colors of the Past

Once was vibrant, now it's faded,
Rainbow dreams that I once traded.
Polka dots have lost their cheer,
Where's that lively pioneer?

Mom's old quilt lays in despair,
Stains of cake and bits of hair.
Frayed edges tell adventures bold,
Of silly times and stories told.

Faded denim from disco days,
Platform shoes in retro craze.
Ripped and worn, but wrinkles smile,
Memories dance in a funky style.

With each stitch a tale of yore,
We laugh, we weep, we love, we soar.
In every patch, the colors blend,
Fading doesn't mean the end.

Breezes of Longing

The wind whispers secrets loud,
Dreams are carried, soft and proud.
Kites are laughing in the sky,
Waving 'bye on breezy high.

Chasing clouds, our hearts take flight,
Socks and shoes are lost in flight.
A gust will snag your favorite hat,
Watch it whirl like a dancing cat!

Longing hearts, they spin around,
In the laughter, love is found.
But where's the kite that spun away?
Screaming clouds as they sway!

So take a leap with giggles free,
Dance with breezes, let it be.
In the laughter, love's sweet song,
Join the winds, where we belong!

Winds of Change in Fabric Form

A squirrel stole a sock from the line,
The neighbors think it's a sign.
With a twist and a whirl,
It'll make quite the twirl!

The gusts laugh as they pull and they sway,
Draped curtains leap in a playful ballet.
While shirts do a tango,
And the pants have a lingo!

Laughter echoes in seams that have split,
As old shirts bemuse with their dance and their wit.
In the breeze they flit,
With every loose bit!

So when the winds giggle and tease,
Remember the fabrics that dance with such ease.
Their fun's not just fluke,
They know how to groove!

Memories on the Margins

An old quilt found in the attic's embrace,
Holds tales of a rat with a knack and a grace.
Each patch a short story,
Of glory, and hoary!

With a coffee stain splash and a mustardy hue,
The fabric insists it’s a tale born anew.
The memories chatter,
Of what’s torn and what’s tattered!

One corner once held a jam sandwich spill,
While a button from grandma lay dormant and still.
They gossip and fumble,
And laugh as they tumble!

The scraps hold the secrets of laughter and cheer,
As they whisper old jokes from yesteryear.
With each frayed edge,
Memories wedge!

Clouds Spun from Memories

Fluffy down quilts float in the air,
As the pillowcases giggle without a care.
They tell tales of dreams,
And of pillow fort schemes!

A breeze with a chuckle sways past the yard,
Unruly the fluffball, it's never too hard.
While laughs chase the light,
In a playful delight!

Every twist in the wind sparks a yarn,
Brought forth from the ages, frayed but not worn.
Like clouds on a spree,
They drift and they free!

So take a moment to cherish the fluff,
Where memories float when the winds get tough.
In puffs of delight,
And laughter so bright!

The Dance of the Unraveled

A ball of yarn loiters in sunlight so grand,
Convinced it's a dancer with moves quite unplanned.
It twirls with a glee,
Like a bee on a spree!

Every needle that pokes brings laughter anew,
As the stitches conspire to take on a view.
They plot under covers,
With threads that are lovers!

As the wind gives a sigh, the needles may bend,
And the yarn takes a leap as it plays with a friend.
Creating a mess,
With flair and finesse!

So watch the entanglement dance through the day,
As laughter undoes what the seamstress gave way.
With each spin and twist,
It flirts like a mist!

Ethereal Strands in Flight

The kites are dancing on a breeze,
With tails that tickle, oh what tease!
They swirl like thoughts without a care,
A game of tag with the open air.

The neighbors laugh, a sight to see,
As one gets stuck in a neighbor's tree.
We rescue it with a lofty cheer,
Then watch it wiggle like it's in a leer.

Around the park, they twist and twirl,
Bright colors flashing, a wondrous whirl.
We shout with glee as one goes free,
While a cat looks on, with a stifled me.

These merry strings, they know no bounds,
Creating joy in playful rounds.
A joyful ride upon the air,
As laughter echoes everywhere!

Serendipity's Gentle Caress

A sock misplaced, now dances bright,
With mismatched flair, a silly sight!
It sways along the garden fence,
In colors bold, it won't make sense.

The cat comes by at just the right time,
To pounce and play, oh what a climb!
A purr and leap, a cotton chase,
A game of hide with each sock's grace.

Wind whispers secrets as they prance,
Socks in the air—a silly dance!
Each flip and twist, a whimsical hug,
As if they're born from a playful mug.

The world smiles wide at this sight so grand,
A joyful ode from nature's hand.
With bearings lost, but spirits high,
In life's sweet chaos, the heart will fly!

The Lilt of Fluttering Hues

Oh, the paper cranes set free from care,
They flutter forth without a dare.
In rainbow hues, they flap and glide,
With mischief written on each side.

A breeze comes roaring with laughter loud,
As cranes collide with a passing cloud.
One spins around, oh what a plight,
She lands right on a chef's hat, what a sight!

The chef just grins, and tosses flour,
That rises up like a fragrant shower.
The cranes are dusted, what a show,
As they take off, now white from toe to toe.

They leave behind a kitchen scene,
Where giggles echo, bright and keen.
With memories formed in a flurry spree,
As laughter floats like birds set free!

Stitches of a Fading Memory

A quilt with patches, stories told,
Each square a memory, some new, some old.
But one patch seems to have slipped away,
As if a ghost asked, “Where’s my play?”

The cat conducts an ensemble grand,
Rolling 'round on a blanket's strand.
He pounces here, with such delight,
As we all laugh at this funny sight.

The laughter fades, the quilt now sings,
Of stitched-together, silly things.
With missing patches, we still weave,
Such joy and chaos, we believe.

So let the patterns dance and sway,
In quirky forms, they’ll find their way.
As memories grow, they’ll never fear,
For laughter’s stitch will always be near!

Weaving Dreams Afloat

In a boat made of fluff,
The seagulls all scoff,
While the fish dance in glee,
As we weave our own spree.

With a needle made of light,
And a sail that’s too tight,
We laugh as we drift,
Chasing whimsical gift.

The stars wear a grin,
As we bob and we spin,
With fabric of laughter,
Creating our own chapter.

So here we will stay,
In our funny ballet,
While the world swirls around,
In our giggles, we're bound.

Wistful Twists of Fate

A floppy hat on my head,
Made from dreams that I've fed,
Like spaghetti, it sways,
In the most silly ways.

The map was a doodle,
With arrows and poodle,
Each twist is a surprise,
As I squint at the skies.

We tumble through time,
In a dance, oh so prime,
With fate's tangled yarn,
Creating glee from the barn.

So let's spin and twirl,
In this whimsical whirl,
With each laugh shared aloud,
We'll bounce through the crowd.

Cascading Fibers of Memory

A spool of bright yarn,
Loops of joy in a barn,
With a cat on my lap,
And a map in my hat.

Unraveling tales slow,
As the north wind will blow,
Each stitch holds a cheer,
In a fabric of fear.

We'll weave in some jokes,
With the quirkiest folks,
As our memories flow,
Like a river of glow.

So let's merrily ply,
Underneath the blue sky,
For the fibers of joy,
Are the things we deploy.

The Lullaby of Unraveled Tales

In a hammock of dreams,
Where the sunlight just beams,
We lay back and sigh,
As the butterflies fly.

With yarn made of whispers,
And stories like sisters,
We'll laugh till we cry,
As the time ticks by.

Each tale has a twist,
In this whimsical mist,
With a wink and a nod,
Life's a playful facade.

So gather 'round near,
With a glass full of cheer,
For the lullaby sings,
Of the joy that it brings.

The Fabric of a Wandering Heart

Stitched with dreams that fray at night,
A fabric dances, oh what a sight!
Buttons pop and threads get loose,
A wandering heart, a playful moose!

Socks mismatched and hats askew,
A patchwork life of me and you.
Fabric soft as jelly beans,
Wandering whims and silly scenes!

Breezy tales on the runway play,
Fashion faux pas in disarray.
But laughter wins; it holds the seam,
In this nonsense, we live our dream!

So wear a smile, let colors clash,
Life's a quilt that makes a splash.
Our wandering hearts, they weave and twirl,
In this hilariously spun world!

Unraveled Stories Under the Sky

Once a story told with flair,
Now it's tangled everywhere.
Under the sky, where clowns compete,
Unraveled tales drop from our feet!

A magician's hat that breathes a sigh,
Out pops a rabbit, oh my, oh my!
With every twist and goofy plot,
We laugh, we forget the tangled knot!

Tales of yarn that never end,
Like socks on a dog, they just pretend!
Each word a stitch, some out of place,
Yet, we cherish this silly space!

At dusk, when stars begin to stretch,
We share our yarns, and they all fetch.
With laughter loud, we pass the time,
Under the sky, life feels like rhyme!

Echoes of Loosely Spun Bonds

Echoes hum where laughter thrives,
Loosely spun, our story jives.
A jump rope frayed in mid-air flight,
Connections sway, what a delight!

With friends like socks from laundry day,
Some are lost, yet love's on display.
A quilt of quirks, mismatched but bold,
Like grandpa's jokes, they never get old!

With each embrace, the yarn unrolls,
Tickling thoughts and silly goals.
Let's weave the tales that tangle tight,
In every laugh, we take our flight!

So spin the yarn and share the gleam,
For echoes live in every dream.
Loosely wound, but heartbeats sound,
In this laughter, our joys abound!

Tapestry of the Floating World

A tapestry blooms, colors collide,
Under the sun, where giggles reside.
Fish in hats and birds in shoes,
In this floating world, we just can't lose!

Kites that spiral, fish that dance,
A riddle of whimsy, a glorious chance.
As clouds wear socks and rivers consort,
Life’s a carnival of wild retorts!

With each pluck, the strings do play,
Echoing laughter, hip-hip-hooray!
In the wind, our spirits twirl,
A guffawing ride through this crazy whirl!

So hold on tight, let chaos reign,
In this tapestry, we find the gain.
With every ruffle and playful bend,
In the floating world, laughter’s our friend!

The Drift of Wayward Ribbons

A ribbon flew high on a gusting breeze,
It twisted and twirled, oh what a tease!
It danced past a squirrel, who gave it a glance,
Then fell on a cat, who missed its great chance.

The kids at the park burst into a cheer,
As the ribbon landed near their big sphere.
They tugged and they pulled, a bright game unfurled,
While the ribbon just laughed, like a con artist girl.

A gentle breeze came, and with a swift dart,
The ribbon broke free, oh, it stole every heart.
It spun round a tree, with a whimsical style,
And left all the onlookers grinning a while.

So, here's to the ribbons that flutter and fly,
With mischief and madness, they catch every eye.
They twirl with delight in the grand summer sun,
A dance of the silly, oh what foolish fun!

Carried Along by Invisible Hands

A sock took a trip, without any mates,
It floated off course, disregarding its fate.
It bumbled and tumbled near puddles of mud,
Where ducks quacked and giggled, oh what a dud!

An errant shoe joined, in a comical chase,
Together they raced with a silly grim face.
They zigged through the grass, then they zapped through a field,
While grasshoppers laughed, their secret revealed.

Now old Mr. Wind had a laugh on his lips,
As the pair of lost items performed clever flips.
The audience chuckled, their glee all around,
As two wayward items waltzed to the sound.

At last they collided with a clear rainbow,
The colors all smiled, as they'd steal the show.
With a whirl and a twirl, they vanished from view,
The charming lost footwear, on their journey so true!

Sunlight on a Tangle of Yarns

A ball of yarn rolled down the bright lane,
It wobbled and bobbled, a colorful train.
With sunlight aglow, it soon met a bee,
Who buzzed with delight, it did not want to flee.

The yarn spun in circles, causing a fuss,
Tangled in petals, oh, what a plus!
A spider peeked out from a web made of dreams,
As the strands intertwined with giggles and screams.

Now, down by the garden, the neighbors all stared,
At the chaos of colors, so brightly compared.
With laughter and glee, they pulled it all tight,
Making sweaters for puppies, oh what a sight!

But soon it unraveled, the yarn in a flurry,
Each piece found a friend, no chance to hurry.
In a tangle we spun, an artful delight,
With sunlight above, the world felt just right!

A Symphony of Wandering Filaments

A feather drifted past a sleeping old cat,
It danced on the breeze, cheeky and sprat.
With a giggle it flew over flowers and bees,
The cat stretched and yawned, just enjoying the tease.

A thread made its entrance, all golden and bold,
It wiggled and jiggled, breaking the mold.
Two playful young kids grabbed hold of the line,
And twirled round in circles, oh how they did shine!

The wind played a tune, a whimsical sound,
As the ducklings all waddled and jumped all around.
Each filament joined in, a whimsical spree,
The world full of laughter, as light as can be.

In the end they all settled, canvas so grand,
Stitched by the memories sewn by the hand.
With joy filling hearts, they gave a great cheer,
To the symphony sung by the friends gathered near!

Nature's Quilt of Secrets

In tattered patches, squirrels dart,
Stitching tales from every part.
A breeze whispers o'er the grass,
As daisies giggle, summers pass.

The trees wear hats of vibrant hues,
Beneath them, ants recite the news.
With butterflies, the gossip spreads,
As cheeky sparrows nod their heads.

Clouds juggle shapes, a circus bold,
While sunbeams thread a tale retold.
The flowers wink and sway about,
As nature’s secrets, laugh and shout.

In this grand quilt, a patchwork plays,
Where every stitch brings sunny days.
So dance and spin, don’t stay still,
For laughter shapes the breeze at will.

Whirling Filaments of Thought

In spinning minds, ideas glide,
Like tumbleweeds that jump and hide.
A thought takes flight on zephyr’s breeze,
And tricks the brain with silly tease.

What if a cloud wore socks today?
Or had a hat that flew away?
A thought of cheese atop a kite,
Makes every afternoon so bright.

In shadows, whispers weave and twist,
Of jellybeans that can't resist.
Ideas dance like fireflies bright,
Will make you giggle through the night.

So let your thoughts take wing and roam,
Through twisted paths that feel like home.
In this mad whirl of crazy dreams,
Life’s fun is stitched in laughter’s seams.

Soft Serenade of Fragments

Where daisies sing to passing bees,
And fallen leaves play tease with breeze.
A serenade of soft delight,
As moody clouds begin to bite.

With cracks in pavements, secret songs,
The neighborhood cats join in along.
Each whisper tells a quirky tale,
Of hiccupping frogs who brazenly wail.

Fragments of laughter float with grace,
As puddles reflect a silly face.
Clouds in a tango, swirling mad,
Make even the grumpiest glad.

So let your smiles drift like puffs,
Each moment filled with gentle guffs.
In this strange dance of joy and cheer,
Every fragment brings life near.

Swaying Patterns of Solitude

In quiet corners, shadows play,
Each whisper soft, a sweet ballet.
A single leaf, it takes a spin,
While lonely crickets start to grin.

The breeze hums low, a gentle tune,
As fireflies gather 'round the moon.
They twirl and jive in patterns grand,
A solo show, all unplanned.

With thoughtful branches swaying high,
They sketch their dreams against the sky.
And every sigh finds laughter's arms,
Embracing all its quirky charms.

So if you're ever feeling lone,
Remember patterns chill to bone.
In solitude, the heart can sway,
And find the fun in every day.

Windborne Fantasies

Up in the air, a sock takes flight,
Chasing a bird in morning light.
A hat joins in, it's lost its pair,
Dancing with joy without a care.

A scarf twirls round like a playful child,
Tickled by breezes, oh so wild.
Laughter spreads through the linen skies,
As breezy pranksters steal the prize.

“Oh look!” cries a mitten with a wink,
“I never thought I’d break the link!”
Fun jumps about on the gusty trails,
A game of tag with no details!

So off they go, a colorful band,
Wandering free, hand in hand.
Their silly frolics bring pure delight,
In the fabric of day, oh what a sight!

Remnants of a Distant Loom

A patch from a quilt now sails like a kite,
Telling tales of warmth, oh what a flight!
A button rolls by with a skip and a hop,
Who needs a jacket when you just can't stop?

A frayed old thread murmurs low,
"Let's start a party, come on, let's go!"
Down by the creek, where the wild things play,
They weave new dreams, come what may.

The tail of a ribbon joins the fun,
Twisting and twirling, oh what a run!
A wild adventure in the fabric of air,
Reviving the past, with flair to spare.

Just then a mitten proclaims with glee,
"This breeze wants to knit, come join me!"
They'll stitch up a storm with laughter and cheer,
As remnants of joy flutter near.

The Hum of Woven Whispers

A tiny napkin flutters and shrieks,
“Oh dear, I’ve lost my way, it stinks!”
A teacup joins in with a cheeky grin,
“Don’t worry, my friend, let's spin and spin!”

Through gusts of laughter, they skedaddle about,
Catching whispers as they twist and shout.
The napkin declares, “I’m a flag of fun!”
While the china chimes, “Let’s dance, everyone!”

The wind carries secrets in a spiraled flight,
Bobbing along in playful delight.
“Yarn balls unite!” calls a mismatched sock,
“Let’s weave a dream, just around the block!”

In a twinkling moment, the sun starts to set,
A confetti of colors, no sign of regret.
Together they spin in a waltz of the breeze,
Creating a song that brings hearts to ease.

An Interlude of Fibers

A spool of yarn lets out a cheer,
"Adventure awaits, I smell it near!"
With a needle in hand, the laughter starts,
Twirling and swirling, they warm their hearts.

A funky patchwork on a mission to play,
Squeezes through clouds, come what may.
A jolly old quilt with memories, bold,
"Let's write new stories as we unfold!"

The buttons jingle with delightful glee,
"Join in, dear fibers, let's cut loose, you'll see!"
A lacy concoction spins in delight,
"Who knew we were stars in this brilliant flight?"

In the midst of it all, a sock screams, "Yay!"
"I'm a superstar finding my way!"
With every gust, they're caught in the rhyme,
An interlude of joy that stands the test of time!

Gossamer Drift

A spider spun a tale, so grand,
It danced on air like no one planned.
With each gust, it took a ride,
Caught in breezes, it just can't hide.

A dog chased after, tail in a swirl,
While cats just watched with a smug twirl.
The fabric of chaos, woven with glee,
A circus of nature, just wait and see.

At picnic tables, napkins took flight,
Sandwiches followed, what a sight!
Lettuce and mustard lost in the spree,
They giggled and rolled like they were free.

The grass whispered secrets, soft and light,
Dandelions scattered, a fluff-filled fight.
On this breezy journey, they wiggled and swayed,
Not a care in the world, oh, how they played!

Celestial Weavings

The moon decided to throw a show,
Stars twinkling in patterns, quite the glow.
One fell from grace, just wanting to dance,
With planets watching, it took a chance.

A comet zoomed past, wearing a hat,
Shooting styles like a playful cat.
While Saturn's rings twirled in delight,
How cosmic chaos sparked through the night.

Asteroids collided with comical flair,
Creating sparks that floated in air.
The universe giggled, turning around,
In this wild ballet, joy was found.

Galaxies twisted, like ribbons they twirled,
In this vast playground, wonders unfurled.
The night sky chuckled, a whimsical plight,
As cosmos conspired to spread pure delight!

Breezy Confessions

A squirrel confessed to a tree so tall,
“Guess what? I’m not collecting nuts at all!”
Acorns scattered, but who would care?
He’d rather play hide and seek in fresh air.

Meanwhile, a crow with a glint in his eye,
Took a stroll on the breeze, oh my, oh my!
“Who needs a job?” he cawed with ease,
“When every gust brings a thrill and a tease.”

The grass whispered tales of mischief tonight,
About dandelions dreaming of flight.
“Bring on the wind!” they shouted as one,
In this hilarious game, they found their fun.

And as fireflies blinked, a party began,
Nature’s own rave, a whimsical plan.
With laughter and sparkles, the night drifted in,
Breezy confessions, where chaos begins!

The Veil of Untold Stories

In a meadow where giggles erupted anew,
A butterfly whispered secrets to dew.
“Did you hear? The wind has a tale!”
As flowers swayed, they turned pale.

The sun spilled laughter, bright and loud,
While clouds gathered in a fluffy crowd.
“Let’s spin a yarn of the things we see,
A tapestry woven, wild and free!”

The trees added riddles, their bark all a chuckle,
With roots that danced in a jubilant shuffle.
“Who’d believe the things that we’ve seen?”
In this vibrant world, every moment’s a dream.

With each gentle breeze, a story took flight,
Mysteries tangled in the soft evening light.
A veil of confusion, wrapped tight with a twirl,
In nature’s embrace, laughter begins to unfurl!

Tapestries in the Breeze

When my socks start to dance, I freeze,
A sock puppet party in the trees.
Spinning round with no sense at all,
Chasing the wind like a lost basketball.

My shirts tumble down like they're on parade,
Making a ruckus, oh, what a charade!
Couch cushions leap, escaping their place,
As if they're winning a whimsical race.

Who knew laundry could giggle so loud?
A humorous mess that draws a proud crowd.
With each twist and turn, spirits run high,
As cloth takes to air, oh me, oh my!

In this playful swirl, all worries take flight,
As garments get giddy, oh what pure delight!
Their road may be bumpy, their journey absurd,
But in this grand fray, every voice is heard.

Unseen Connections

I found a cat that wore a hat,
With feathers and flares, imagine that!
He pranced about with flair and grace,
Saying, 'I'm the king of this wild place!'

The dog, bemused, gave him a glance,
And wagged his tail, asked for a dance.
But hats and paws make a funny team,
As they twirled around in a wild dream.

Neighbors stopped to sip some tea,
While critters pranced, as wild as can be.
These curious pals blend fun with cheer,
Each wag and pounce makes joy appear.

A mouse donned a sash, oh what a sight,
As the trio laughed into the night.
In a world so silly, connections so grand,
It's clear the fun is never quite planned.

Silhouettes of Loomed Memories

In grandma's attic, dust bunnies play,
Woven delights from a distant day.
They whisper stories of fabric and thread,
While sporting lace hats on their fuzzy heads.

Uncle's old pants start a new trend,
With patches and colors that seem to blend.
"Fashion's a cycle!" they all seem to say,
As they strut down the hall in a funny ballet.

The curtains get frisky with the rhythm of air,
Dancing like friends, without a care.
They giggle and sway with their patterned flair,
As shadows perform in a zany affair.

Mismatched socks join into the fray,
Twirling in circles, come what may.
It's a fabric festival, a grand curtsy shout,
In the loom of memories, laughter's the route.

Fragile Whims of the Past

Old toys rattle as dust meets the light,
Each one a memory, a giggling delight.
A doll with a smile, so silly and wide,
Sipping lemonade on a fluffy cloud ride.

The baseball bat winks with a cheeky spin,
Recalling the days of "Let's come on in!"
As marbles roll forward, a quirky ballet,
Each color a giggle in the warm sun's ray.

Jokes in the closet, they whisper and cackle,
As shadows of humor continue to tackle.
Amidst the forgotten, soft laughter prevails,
In the silly remnants of childhood trails.

So let us revive those whimsical days,
With fragile wishes that continue to play.
For every joke told and each smile that passed,
It spins us together, a fun-loving cast.

Currents of Forgotten Weaves

In the attic, dust bunnies play,
Frolicking subjects of yesterday's fray.
Exploring lost patterns with glee,
Laughing at mem'ries like old family trees.

Socks paired with a hat, how bizarre,
A dance of oddities, the latest star.
Jumping around, the knitting's confused,
Fashion's new style, slightly amused.

Cords from the vacuum, tangled and bright,
Sing a duet in the soft morning light.
Caught in a whirlwind, they twist and they turn,
In this comic fabric, what more can we learn?

The cat joins the party in awkward delight,
Chasing the ribbons that dart in a flight.
As we watch the show from our comfortable spots,
We giggle at fate and its curious knots.

Whispered Dreams on the Breeze

A kite from the fair, now lost to the sky,
Elopes with the clouds, oh my, oh my!
Balloons filled with laughter, floating along,
Singing to the world, a whimsical song.

Old ladies on porches in hats shaped like pies,
Chuckle as sparrows steal remnants of fries.
A hat that's too big tips over their eyes,
They cackle and giggle at gullible lies.

Swirling umbrellas caught in a gust,
Dance like they're partners in a waltz, oh, trust!
Raccoons in tuxedos conduct a parade,
As we laugh at the spectacle that fate has made.

Pigeons judging fashion with overly stern looks,
At squirrels crafting nests with old gardening books.
Nature's own humor, in every small thing,
Whispers of joy that the breezes will bring.

The Flute of Woven Whispers

A noodle escapes from diner's delight,
And swims through the air, a daring flight.
Pasta in mid-air, doing a pirouette,
The chef drops his spoon, gives a bemused fret.

The spaghetti guitar strums a silly tune,
As broccoli boogies beneath the bright moon.
Fishsticks wearing hats, they dance in a line,
While carrots compete in a rather sly vine.

The kitchen’s a circus with all kinds of flair,
As forks take a bow and the spoons do declare,
Salad spins wildly, forgetting its dress,
In a concert of chaos, culinary mess.

With laughter like bubbles, the evening does shine,
As mashed potatoes roll, in this bistro divine.
A whimsical symphony, the flavors unite,
Oh, the silly serenade of food takes flight!

Hidden Patterns in the Air

A cat on a leash, strutting so proud,
Makes the softest landing in midair, unbowed.
Dogs look confused, as if in a dream,
Praise to the feline, a curious team.

The squirrels hold meetings on top of a fence,
Debating the merits of common sense.
With acorns as currency, they make their deals,
While birds on the wire chime in with squeals.

Life’s tapestry wobbles in whimsical sway,
As shadows do tango at the end of the day.
Clouds wear katana, slicing at gloom,
In this jester's domain, we all find our room.

The wind it does giggle, a mischievous gale,
Adventurous leaves, like sails, set to sail.
So take off your hat, let the laughter unfurl,
In this topsy-turvy and whimsical swirl.

Notes of a Wandering Stitch

In a fabric shop, I lost my way,
Stitching llamas on a bright blue sway.
Buttons laughed as I stumbled near,
Who knew fabric could bring such cheer?

Sewing bees buzzing all around,
One tried to make my needle drown.
I giggled at a thread so long,
Thought I'd sing it a little song!

Patches argue on who's the best,
While I'm just trying to get some rest.
An apron winked with a cheeky smile,
"Let's have fun, just stay awhile!"

So here's to stitches that jiggle and twist,
And all the fabric I can't resist.
May my journey be a playful ride,
With every stitch, let joy reside!

Featherlight Connections Under the Stars

Under the sky with a blanket spread,
I saw a pillow fight, ‘twas a featherbed.
Stars winked down, “Join in the fun!”
But feathers tangled ‘til I couldn’t run!

A sock danced freely under the moon,
While a quilt hummed its favorite tune.
Laughter swirled through the cozy air,
As a rogue button proposed a dare!

They whispered secrets, soft and light,
Casting shadows in the cool night.
“Let’s thread the night with giggles galore,
And patch our dreams, oh, who could ask for more?”

So here I am, in stitches and glee,
Enjoying friendships with fabric, you see.
Under the stars, all worries dispelled,
As featherlight ties of joy are held!

The Art of Letting Go

Once in a basket, a yarn ball sat,
It dreamed of colors, oh imagine that!
But with each tug, it started to fray,
“Let me unwind!” it begged in dismay.

A snip here, a snip there, I took a chance,
And soon it tumbled into a dance.
“I’m free!” it yelled, “Don’t hold me back,
I want to twist and create my own track!”

Knots tried to bind it, like old shoe laces,
But laughter spread through those fuzzy spaces.
With every roll, it found its way,
Becoming new art in bright array!

So here’s to yarn balls that break the rules,
Who teach us letting go can be cool.
With joy in their dance, they show us the flow,
Embracing the chaos in the art of ‘go.’

Flickers of Light Upon Untamed Fibers

In a craft store, I found a bright thread,
It flickered and danced, “Come join me,” it said.
Buttons cheered, and fabric swirled,
In a wild dance, creativity unfurled!

A clothespin waved from its wooden perch,
“Let’s make some magic, put on a search!”
So I gathered yarns of every hue,
Chasing colors that sang, “Look at you!”

With fibers untamed, we stitched a tale,
Of silly puns and a bouncing snail.
As laughter echoed, the fabric sighed,
In playful chaos, joy always bides!

So here’s to flickers that bring us together,
With all of life’s fibers, let loose and tether.
For in this dance of the wild and free,
We find delight in each stitch of glee!

Fragments Blown Afield

A sock flew high upon a breeze,
Chasing after wayward bees.
It danced and twirled in bright daylight,
Nomadic wanderer in sight.

Old hats laugh as they take a spin,
A feathered friend can't hold it in.
They twirl through trees and laugh with glee,
Oh look, there's Gerald, rolling free!

A scarf unfurls, a silly sight,
Like a superhero in mid-flight.
It wraps around a random man,
Who grins and laughs, "I've got a plan!"

So join the fun, don't stay confined,
Where laughter mixes with the wind.
These fragments blown, oh what a scene,
Floating freely, ever keen.

The Art of Airy Weavings

A rogue balloon escapes the bag,
A prancing pal, a playful wag.
It bobs and weaves, a jester's dance,
Inviting all to join its chance.

A kite gets jealous, flaps its tail,
Determined now to dance and sail.
They twist and dodge in sheer delight,
Who knew the sky could be so bright?

With sticks and strings, a feathery show,
Spinning shapes like a magic flow.
Grandmas chuckle, they sip their tea,
At the great airborne jamboree!

So grab your hat, don’t stay too long,
Embrace the wind, join in the song.
With every drift, we set the morn,
In this circus of fabric, reborn.

Whimsical Breezes and Twisted Yarns

A silly sunbeam’s making rounds,
Bouncing off the laundry grounds.
It giggles as the shirts all sway,
Belly laughing at their play.

A rogue pair of undies takes a leap,
Whirling ‘round, they cannot keep.
The neighbors peek with chuckles wide,
“Is that a dance or undie pride?”

Socks become the strongest team,
United in a lofty dream.
They flutter, swirl, and spin, oh my!
Chasing clouds through the blue sky.

So let them twirl and make their mark,
In wind's fair game, they leave their spark.
With fabrics cheery, join the fun,
In this whimsy, we all are one!

Threads Untangled in Flight

A rogue piece of string decides to flee,
Twisting ‘round a happy tree.
It tangles birds and kites galore,
A raucous scene, the trees implore!

An old vest caught, how quaint indeed,
It joins the party, feels the need.
With buttons bouncing, oh what glee,
They’re all now best friends with the tree!

A mischievous breeze swoops down to play,
Wrapping up all in its frolic way.
Oh, who knew fabrics could delight,
In a tussle ‘neath the warming light!

So let the fun unfold in air,
Let fabrics tumble, twist, and share.
In this grand dance, we find our prose,
In laughter’s warmth, the magic grows.

Hopes Tattered by Time

Once I had dreams, all shiny and bold,
Now they're like socks, with holes that unfold.
I chase silly wishes, like butterflies rare,
But they flutter away, as if they don't care.

Life's a jumble, a quirky old trip,
I trip over laughter and land on my hip.
With fortune like noodles, all tangled and twist,
I giggle through mishaps, not once have I missed.

Old plans are like kites, caught up in a tree,
I shrug and I giggle; oh woe is not me!
For every odd turn is a chance to spin round,
In the circus of life, I'm quite the clown found.

So here's to the days that don't go as we scheme,
I'll dance like a jester, I'll laugh and I'll beam.
With hopes ever tattered, but joy still intact,
I'll gather my humor, and that's a good fact.

A Dance of Whimsy and Yarn

In a yarn shop of dreams, where colors collide,
I wove a wild tangle, no reason nor guide.
With every odd loop, a dance began,
Spinning tales of mischief, oh what a plan!

I twirled with a kitten, on two lefty feet,
She tangled my laces, oh silly sweet treat.
While stitches were popping, and yarn flew around,
We became the duo that laughter had found.

A scarf turned to spaghetti, all slurped in delight,
We twirled through the chaos, giggling through night.
With colors ablaze, we painted the room,
Making memories bright, from joy and from gloom.

So if you feel frumpy, come join in the fun,
With whimsy and yarn, we'll dance 'til we're done.
In this world of the quirky, may laughter be spun,
For even in chaos, we know we have won!

Elusive Threads of Destiny

I peeked out the window, a fortune in sight,
A chance for a win, or a pie fight delight.
But destiny giggled, and waved me along,
With options as strange as a cat in a thong.

I tossed out my wishes like seeds in the breeze,
They sprouted odd fruits, and gave me a tease.
Each pluck led to laughter, each turn was a jest,
With fates that were sillier than I'd ever guessed.

A pickle in slippers, a banana on skates,
These were my buddies, and all their sweet traits.
In the garden of whimsy, we circled and spun,
While the sun shone on chaos, and shadows forgone.

So if life's got you reeling, just join in the chase,
With odd little friends, and a smile on your face.
We'll dance through the day, with each wobble and fling,
In this timeless adventure, we're destined to sing!

Knots in the Gentle Wind

The wind made a fuss, with a knot in its stride,
It tickled and teased, as it twisted and sighed.
With each silly puff, my hat took to flight,
I chased it down alleys, oh what a sight!

Tangled in laughter, I stumbled and spun,
Like a fool in a circus, I'm never outdone.
I caught it at last, with a triumph so bold,
But it laughed back at me, freedom not sold!

Umbrellas went flipping, and scarves took their chance,
To join in the frolic, a playful dance.
With giggles and shouts, I let go of my woes,
Each twist in the breeze, a new story arose.

So here's to the knots that we stumble upon,
A reminder that life isn't meant to be drawn.
With joy in each knot, and humor unfurled,
I'll embrace all the chaos this windy world.

Lifting Stitches from the Earth

From soil below, a needle leaps,
It dances high, where laughter creeps.
A patchwork quilt, the daisies sigh,
As socks get lost, they wonder why.

Unruly threads, they twist and twine,
In chaos found, a punchline's shine.
A tangle here, a tumble there,
A sewing bee with bolts of flair.

A squirrel dons a woolen cap,
While rabbits giggle in a lap.
The earth itself, a seamstress grand,
With stitches sewn across the land.

And when it rains, we hear the glee,
Of splashes bright, like jubilee.
Each droplet laughs, a playful game,
As nature's fabric gets its fame.

The Essence of Tangled Reminisce

Nostalgia’s threads have taken flight,
They loop and swirl, creating sight.
A frolic of the yesteryear,
Where every snicker draws you near.

A hat misplaced, a scarf astray,
In corners where the light will play.
Old photos burst with life anew,
In every smile, a twist or two.

The past can dance, if just allowed,
In every yarn, a joyful crowd.
We skip along this woven path,
In patterns bright, we find our laugh.

So grab a stitch, and hold it tight,
In every twist, find pure delight.
These silly threads, a tale to spin,
A joyful journey to begin.

Curved Lines of Memory

A winding road in gentle curves,
Where tangled thoughts do swish and swerve.
An old dog barks at passing kites,
While kittens nap in their delights.

The yarnball rolls, it takes a spin,
As memories tug, we reel them in.
A slide, a swing, a joyful cheer,
In every nook, a chuckle's near.

A garden party with quirky hats,
Where ants conspire and gossip bats.
The sun sets low with golden gleam,
Each moment's stitched into the dream.

So dance, dear heart, in arcs and loops,
With laughter echoing, skip with woops!
In winding paths, our spirits soar,
In every line, a giggle's core.

Swirling Echoes of the Unknown

In shadows cast by pups at play,
Curiosities lead astray.
Echoes giggle, they skip and joke,
As whispers twist, and tomfoolery awoke.

A whoopee cushion, a prankish squeak,
Turns serious faces to laughter's peak.
With swirling mists to guide the fun,
The unknown giggles, a race begun.

Balloons float high, like dreams unbound,
While dirt-filled shoes dance on the ground.
With each burst laugh, a secret shared,
In swirling arcs, we've all prepared.

So let the echoes spiral wide,
With sharp punches and silly pride.
In every laugh, we break the mold,
With crazy calls of spirits bold.

Threads of Time Unspooled

A sock has vanished in the wash,
It dances now with paper squashes.
The clock ticks slowly, yet I find,
It's just lost time that’s unaligned.

My sweater gained a surprising hole,
Did a mouse turn it into a bowl?
Or did the cat just need a toy,
That made me laugh, oh what a joy!

The fabric of my life is strange,
With every twist, there’s room to change.
Each stitch a story, quite absurd,
In yarns of mishaps, I’ve concurred.

Now as the fibers all unwind,
I giggle at what I once designed.
For life’s a fabric, wild and free,
Laughing at yarns, it’s meant to be!

Fleeting Stitches of the Heart

A thread that binds two hearts in jest,
Can fray and tangle at its best.
Why does my heart feel like a glove,
That can’t quite catch the things I love?

In moments fleeting, love may slip,
Like butter in a mid-summer dip.
We laugh and chase like silly fools,
With love as light as trippy mules.

Each joke we share a quirky seam,
In laughter’s art, we find our dream.
Though stitches break, we're still a pair,
In patchwork joy beyond compare.

So as we sew our days with cheer,
I’ll keep you close, oh dear, oh dear!
A clumsy knot, but that’s the way,
We dance through life, come what may.

Ethereal Patterns

The wind brings whispers, quite a twist,
It knits in patterns we can’t resist.
I saw a bird with a scarf so bright,
It flapped and teased throughout the night.

Balloons float high, with strings that tangle,
While I pursue my own sweet jangle.
Laughter echoes as kites entwine,
In this grand game of fate and line.

Chasing clouds that wear a crown,
I trip on sunlight, almost drown.
A fairy’s laughter sprinkled in,
With every flip, the giggles spin.

So I embrace this whirly dance,
With every twirl, there lies a chance.
For in this chaos, joy’s the prize,
A wobbly quilt ‘neath sunny skies!

Echoing the Unseen

A ghostly thread glides with a wink,
Invisible yet makes us think.
It pulls our laughs and hides our sighs,
In shadows play where humor lies.

I tossed a paper plane and jumped,
But it just twirled and lightly thumped.
Did it explore the skies so grand,
Or land somewhere in a stranger's hand?

The echoes of the nighttime jest,
In unseen paths we find our fest.
Chasing giggles through the dark,
With every night, there's a new spark.

Though unseen, these moments stay,
With laughter, light, they pave the way.
So let us dance in laughter’s sheen,
In this fine mess of the unseen!

www.ingramcontent.com/pod-product-compliance
Lightning Source LLC
Chambersburg PA
CBHW050304120526
44590CB00016B/2483